Yiddish Wisdom *for* Parents

Library of Congress Cataloging-in-Publication Data available.

ISBN 0-8118-3101-9

Note on the translation and transliteration.
Translation is the process of turning or rendering one language
into another. Transliteration is the process of rendering phonetically
the sound of one language with the letters of another language.
The transliterated words in this volume are a very close approximation
to the pronunciation of Yiddish words using the system developed by
the YIVO (Yiddish Scientific Institute). The acronym YIVO is a
transliteration of the first letters in the four Yiddish words that make
up the name of the organization.
—R. M.

Printed in Singapore

Designed by Kirsten T. Hetland

Distributed in Canada by Raincoast Books
9050 Shaughnessy Street
Vancouver, British Columbia V6P 6E5

10 9 8 7 6 5 4 3 2 1

Chronicle Books LLC
85 Second Street
San Francisco, California 94105

www.chroniclebooks.com

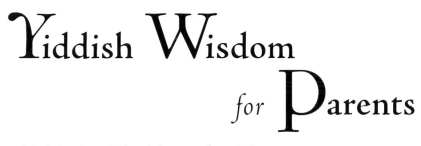

Yiddish Wisdom for Parents

Yiddishe Khokhme far Eltern

ILLUSTRATIONS BY
KRISTINA SWARNER

TRANSLATION AND INTRODUCTION BY
RAE MELTZER

CHRONICLE BOOKS
SAN FRANCISCO

Yiddish grew from a blend of Hebrew fragments and local German dialects in Europe's Rhine Valley about 1000 years ago. Although both Hebrew and Yiddish share the same characters, each has a separate vocabulary, history, and linguistic structure.

As the Jews of the Rhine Valley migrated they took Yiddish with them. Contact with Slavic-speakers introduced Slavic elements, loosening Yiddish's roots in medieval German, and further migration has introduced words from neighboring languages such as Russian, Polish, Czechoslovakian, Latvian, Lithuanian, and other European tongues. Similarly, as Yiddish has drawn from these languages, Yiddish words and phrases have been incorporated into other languages, such as *shlep* [to drag], *kibbitz* [to joke], and *beygl* ["bagel"] in American English.

Yiddish proverbs are found throughout Yiddish literature, especially in the writing of Sholem Aleykhem and, more recently, in the work of Isaac Bashevis Singer, who also recited in Yiddish his acceptance speech for the 1978 Nobel Prize for Literature. Today, there seems to be a resurgence of interest, something of a delicate renaissance, in Yiddish: U.S. college and university campuses are offering courses in the language, as are many Jewish communities.

The cultural traditions of the Jewish people have always centered on parents and children, and the responsibility of parents to raise and educate their children is one of the highest priorities of the Jewish family. This book collects words of wisdom for parents in proverbs—universal, colorful, sometimes surprising—handed down to us through centuries of Jewish culture and history. Held in their wise words are the joys and bafflements, pride, worries, warmth, and wonders of raising children.

—*Rae Meltzer*

✻

Teach a child in the way he
should go, and when he is old he
will not depart from it.

Lernt a kind in der veg vi er zol geyn, un ven er iz alt
vet er nit opgeyn fun dem.

✻

**If you must beat a child,
use a string.**

Oyb du muzt shlogn a kind, nuts di shnirl.

❈

**The apple doesn't fall
far from the tree.**

Dos epl falt nit vayt fun boym.

**Not to teach your son to work
is like teaching him to steal.**

Nit tsu lernen dayn zun tsu arbetn iz glaykh
vi lernen im tsu ganvenen.

※

**The talk of the child in
the street is like the talk of his
father or mother at home.**

Dos vos a kind redt in gas iz vos zayn tate
oder mame reydn in der heym.

Don't threaten a child; either
punish him or forgive him.

Strashe nit a kind; oder bashtroft im oder fargeb im.

❊

Though parents have a dozen
children, each is the only one.

Khotsh eltern hobn a tuts kinder, yeder iz
der eyntsik eyns.

❊

It is hard to raise sons and
much harder to raise daughters.

Es iz shver tsu hodeven zin nor a sakh shverer
tsu hodeven tekhter.

**When it comes to his children,
every parent is blind.**

Ven es kumt tsu eygne kinder, zaynen ale eltern blind.

❀

**One mother achieves more than
a hundred teachers.**

Eyn mame dergreykht mer vi a hundert lerers.

**Small children, a headache;
big children, a heartache.**

Kleyne kinder, a kopveytik; groyse kinder, hartsveytik.

❖

**What you learn in childhood
is proven true in old age.**

Dos vos du lernst in kindhayt vet zikh dervayzn
tsu zayn emes in der elter.

❖

**At different ages, a person
feels differently.**

In farsheydene yorn hot men andershe gefiln.

There's no rain without thunder, and children are not born without pain.

Es ken nit zayn kayn regen on duner, un kinder kenen nit geboyrn vern on veytik.

* * *

A daughter confides only in her mother.

A tokhter fargleybt nor in ir mame.

* * *

Like father, like son.

Vi der tate, azoy der zun.

Little people don't travel far.

Kleyne layt geyn nit vayt.

Parents shouldn't praise
their own children; no one
will believe them.

Tate-mame darfn zeyere kinder nit loybn,
vayl keyner vet zey nit gloybn.

✿

The rich don't have children;
they have heirs.

Di gevirim hobn nit kinder; zey hobn yorshim.

✿

Little children have big ears.

Kleyne kinder hobn groyse oyern.

Once parents used to teach
their children to talk;
today children teach their
parents to keep quiet.

Amol flegn di eltern lernen di kinder redn; haynt
lernen di kinder di eltern shvaygn.

When the father supports
his son, both laugh; but when
the son supports his father,
both cry.

Az der tate vet helfn dem zun, lakhn beyde; az der zun
vet helfn dem tate veynen beyde.

It is better to have nobility of character than nobility of birth.

Es iz beser hobn eydlkayt fun kharakter vi zayn
eydl geborn.

❀

**Never promise something
to a child and not give it
to him, because in that way he
learns to lie.**

Keyn mol tsuzog epes tsu dem kind un gib es nit tsu im,
vayl azoy vet er oyslernen vi tsu lign.

If you don't teach the ox to plow when he is young, it will be difficult to teach him when he is grown.

Oyb du vest nit lernen dem oxs tsu akern az er iz yung, vet zayn zeyer shver im oyslernen az er iz dervaksn.

❋

Children without a childhood are tragic.

Kinder on kindhayt zynen tragish.

Good manners supersede learning.

Gute manirn farnemen dem ort fun toyre.

❖

A father's good deeds are a good example for his son.

A tate's gute mitsves zaynen a guter
bayshpil for zayn zun.

Bearing children is difficult,
raising them even more so.

Hobn kinder iz shver ober hodeven zey iz nokh shverer.

❉

Joy from children is more
precious than money.

Nakhes fun kinder iz mer tayer far gelt.

✻

**My father planted for me
and I plant for my children.**

Mayn tate hot farzeyt far mir un
ikh farzey far mayne kinder.

✻

**When you teach your son,
you also teach your grandson.**

Ven du lernst dayn zun, lernst du oykh dayn eynikl.

❊

Became so isn't born so.

Gevorn iz nit geborn.

❊

**To be a parent takes know-how,
but everyone takes it on anyhow.**

Tsu zayn tate-mame iz a kunst,
ober ale nemen es unter, say vi say.

A good daughter makes a good daughter-in-law.

A gute tokhter makht a gute shnur.

❖

Children grow up, parents grow old.

Kinder vaksn oys, eltern vern alt.

❖

A mother is like a veil: she hides the faults of her children.

A mame iz vi a dektikhl:
zi fardekt di khesroynes fun di kinder.

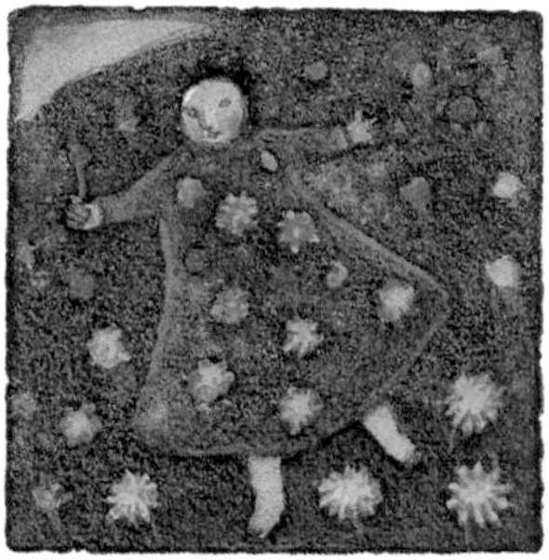

Like garden, like gardener.

Glaykh der gortn, glaykh der gertner.

**Whom God would punish,
he sends bad children.**

Vemen Got vil bashtrofn, shikt er shlekhte kinder.

What God is to the world,
parents are to their children.

Vos Got iz tsu der velt, eltern zaynen tsu zeyere kinder.

✤

Since God could not be
everywhere, he created mothers.

Zint Got ken nit zayn umetum, hot er geshafn mames.

✤

Knowledge obtained in
childhood is not forgotten.

Dos visn vos men krigt fun kindhayt,
fargest men nit.

The least demanding child
is easily neglected.

Di shtile kind ken men fargesn.

✻

To every mother her children
are the most successful.

Tsu yeder mame zaynen ire kinder gerotene.

There can never be
too many drinking glasses
or too many children.

Kinder un glezer hot men keyn mol nit tsu fil.

The eggs teach the hens.

Di eyer lernen di hiner.

❈

A child's wisdom is also wisdom.

A kind's khokhme iz oykhet khokhme.

❈

The shoes of the poor man's child grow with their feet.

Di shikh fun dem oreman's kind vaksn mitn fisl.

❖

Parents can provide everything except good luck.

Eltern kenen alts gebn, nor kayn mazl kenen
zey nit gebn.

**From bad matches can come
good children.**

Fun krume shiddukhim kenen aroys
kumen glaykhe kinder.

✻

**All fingers hurt equally
and all children are equally dear
to their parents.**

Ale finger tuen glaykh vey un ale kinder
zaynen glaykh tayer.

Children bring good fortune,
children bring misfortune.

Kinder brengen glik, kinder brengen umglik.

✣

If the world will ever be
redeemed, it will be only through
the merit of children.

Oyb di velt vet amol vern derlayzn, vet es zayn nor
durkh dem fardinen fun kinder.

✣

What the old chew,
the young spew.

Vos di alte kayen, di yunge shpayen.

The warmest bed is mother's.

Di varemste bet is di mame's.

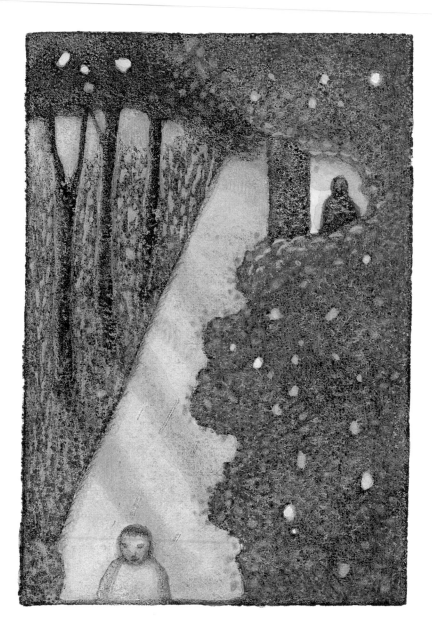

✻

Small children don't
let you sleep; big children
don't let you rest.

Kleyne kinder lozn nit shlofn; groyse kinder
lozn nit ruen.

✻

**With a child in the house,
all corners are full.**

Mit a kind in shtub, zaynen ale vinkelehk farnumen.

※

**When a girl is born, it's a
success for the family.**

Ven es vert geborn a meydl, iz es a hatslokhe far der
mishpokhe.

※

**If you're still a child
at twenty, you're an ass
at twenty-one.**

Az men iz biz tsvantsik your nokh alts a kind,
iz men an eyzl tsu eyn-un-tsvantsik.

A child's tears reach
the heavens.

Di trern fun a kind dergreykhn tsum himl.

❈

For the sake of one's
children, parents would tear
apart a world.

Far kinder veln eltern tsuraysn a velt.

**There is no such thing as
a bad mother.**

Es iz nito aza zakh vi a shlekhte mame.

❊

**A young tree bends; an old
tree breaks.**

A yunger boym beygt zikh; an alter
boym brekht zikh.

Before you utter a word
you're a wise man, afterward
you're a fool.

Eyder me zogt aroys a vort, iz men a khokhem,
dernokh is men a nar.

❊

If a daughter has no other
virtues, even a freckle can be
considered a virtue.

Az di tokhter hot nit kayn ondere mayles,
is a zumer-shprinkle oykh a mayle.

❖

Every mother thinks her child is beautiful.

Yeder mame denkt az ir kind iz sheyn.

❖

**Children and money make
a nice world.**

Kinder un gelt makhn a sheyne velt.

⁂

**As one is at seven, so is one
at seventy.**

Vi eyner iz tsu zibn, azoy iz er tsu zibetsik.

**Three things grow overnight:
profits, rent, and girls.**

Dray zakhn vaksn iber nakht:
revokhim, diregelt, un meydlakh.

✿

**For the disease of stubbornness
no cure exists.**

Far dem kronkhayt fun akshnkayt iz nito kayn refue.

**God never told anyone
to be stupid.**

Got hot keynmol gezogt emetsn zayn narish.

✣

**One father can support
ten children; but it is difficult
for ten children to support
one father.**

Eyn tate ken oys'haltn tsen kinder; ober es iz shver
for tsen kinder tsu oys'haltn eyn tate.

**Little children, little joys;
big children, big worries.**

Kleyne kinder, kleyne freydn; groyse kinder,
groyse zorgn.

✺

**Learning cannot be bequeathed
or inherited.**

Toyre can men nit opshraybn oder beyerushe.

If the pupil is smart, the teacher
is praised.

Az der talmid iz a khokhem, iz der lerer farloybt.

✤

Eggs may be smarter than hens,
but soon they begin to smell.

Eyer zaynen efsher kliger far hiner,
ober bald shtinken zey.

✤

Without family life, no nation
can be built.

On mishpokhe lebn, ken men a land un a folk nit boyen.

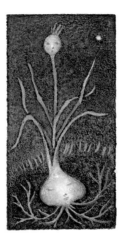

Fruits take after their roots.

Frukht zaynen azoy vi zeyere vortslen.

❖

※

**Each child carries his own
blessing into the world.**

Yeder kind trogt zayn eygne brokhe arayn in der velt.

※

He who teaches a child is as if he had created him.

Der vos lernt a kind iz azoy vi er
hot im bashafn.

❧

A dog is sometimes more faithful than a child.

A hunt iz amol getrayer fun a kind.

❧

In youth a donkey; in old age an ass.

In der yugnt an eyzl; oyf der elter a beheyme.

**My children, big and small,
are all prodigies.**

Mayne kinder, di kleyne un de groyse,
zaynen ale vunderkinder.

✻

**Little children are held in
one's arms; big children are
a worry on one's mind.**

Kleyne kinder halt men oyf di hent; groyse kinder
zaynen a zorg in zinen.

Whoever does not try, does not learn.

Ver es vet nit prubirn, vet nit lernen.

❖

No person is too old to learn.

Keyner iz nit tsu alt tsu lernen.

To obey out of love is better
than to obey out of fear.

Tsu folgn tsulib libe iz beser eyder folgn tsulib shrek.

❊

Like the mother,
so is the daughter.

Vi di mame, azoy iz di tokhter.

❊

A wise son makes his
father glad; a foolish son is the
grief of his mother.

A kluger zun makht zayn tate tsufridn; a narisher zun is
der troyer fun der mame.

To seek wisdom in old age
is like a mark in the sand.
To seek wisdom in youth is like
engraving on stone.

Tsu zukhn khokhme in der elter is vi
a tseykhn in zamd; tsu zukhn khokhme in yugnt
iz vi gravyrn oyf a shteyn.

❋

Experience is what
we call the accumulation
of our mistakes.

Iberlebungen iz dos vos men ruft dem onklaybnzam
fun unzere toesn.

Those who do not grow, grow smaller.

Di vos vaksn nit, vern kleyner.

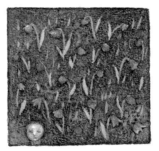

He who acquires knowledge
without imparting it to others is
like a flower in the desert where
there is no one to enjoy it.

Der was hot dos visn un git dos nit iber tsu
ondere iz vi a blum in dem midber vu dort is keyner
tsu hobn fargenign fun blum.

✺

Blessed is the son who studies
with his father, and blessed is
the father who teaches his son.

Gebentsht iz der zun vos shtudirt mit zayn tate, un
gebentsht iz der tate vos lernt zayn zun.

Losing teeth and bearing children ages one fast.

Farlirn tseyn un hobn kinder vert men shnel alt.

✿

Don't fret over married children; they will take care of themselves.

Zorgt nit iber ayere farheyrate kinder; zey kenen akhtung gebn oyf zikh.

Let the calf run; it will come home when it's hungry.

Loz dos kalb loyfn; es vet aheym kumen ven es vet zikh oys-hungern.

✶

From the lowly potato you get the tastiest pancake.

Fun a proste bulbe kumt aroys di geshmakste latke.

**For raising children you
need Rothschild's wealth and
Samson's strength.**

Hodeven kinder muz men hobn Rothschild's raykhkayt
un Shimshon's shtarkayt.

❊

**With a daughter you're busy
all your life.**

Mit a tokhter iz men farnumen a gants lebn.

❀

One's own is beloved.

Vos iz eygn iz balibt.

❀

**What one spoils in youth
cannot be repaired by age.**

Vos men makht kalye in yugnt, ken men
oyf der elter nit farikhtn.

✻

**A mother's tears, a father's cuff,
prove useful in this life.**

Mame's trern un tate's shmits kumen shtark
tsu nuts in lebn.

**He that has children
in the cradle should not quarrel
with the world.**

Ver es hot kinder in vig, zol zikh nit
krign mit der velt.

*

**Even a child is known
by his deeds.**

Afile a kind iz bavust durkh zayne mitsves.

A strict master will not have understanding sons.

A shtrenger mayster vet nit hobn farshteyndike zin.

⁕

First learn, then teach.

Ersht lern zikh, un dan lernen ondere.

⁕

Don't gossip about other children while yours are still growing up.

Ir zolt nit baredn ondere kinder, vayle ayere kinder vaksn nokh oys.

Don't limit a child to your
own knowledge, for he was born
in another time.

Halt nit a kind tsu ayr egenem visn, vayle, er iz geboyrn
gevorn in an onder tsayt.

*

A mother's curse uproots
the young plant.

A mame's klole ken oysvortslen di yunge geviks.

**A child without a pacifier is like
a door without a knob.**

A kind on a smotshik iz vi a tir on a kliamke.

***

Wisdom comes with the years.

Khokhme kumt mit di yorn.

**Little ones don't let you
chew; big ones don't let you
buy anything new.**

Kleyne lozn nit kayen; groyse lozn
nit koyfn gornisht nay.

❧

With anger you don't get too far.

Mit kaas geyt men nit tsu vayt.

❧

Goofy goose, goofy goslings.

Fardreyte gandz, fardreyte gendzl.

Kindness is remembered,
meanness gives an ache in
the heart.

Gut'hartsikayt gedenkt men, shlekhts
tut vey in harts.

❖

Be quick to listen, and respond
patiently and wisely.

Zay shnel tsu oys' hern, un entver mit geduld
un mit khokhme.

❖

Better that the child should cry
than the father.

Beser az dos kind zol veynen eyder der tate.

If you do not honor your parents, your children will not honor you.

Oyb du vest nit gebn koved tsu dayne eltern,
veln dayne kinder nit gebn koved tsu dir.

The follies of children are termites to their father's possessions.

Di narishkayt fun kinder zaynen termitn
tsu zayer tate's farmegns.

✻

Blood is thicker than water.

Blut iz diker fun vaser.

✻

**A refined girl is a little dove
when she becomes a wife.**

Di eydle meydl iz a kleyne taybl ven zi vert a vaybl.

❀

**That which is practiced in youth
will be pursued in old age.**

Dos vos men praktitsirt in yugnt, vet men
ton in der elter.

❀

**Having one child is like
having one eye.**

Ayn kind is ozoy vi eyn oyg.

Whatever a child babbles, his
mother will understand.

Vos a kind vet palplen vet zayn mame farshtayn.

✿

When a son gets married
he gives his wife a contract and
makes his mother a divorcee.

Ven der zun hot khasene git er zayn vayb a kontrakt
un makht zayn mame a grushe.

✿

The highest wisdom is kindness.

Di hekhste khokhme iz gut'hartsikayt.

If one has children, health, and money, life will be sunny.

Az men hot kinder, gezunt un gelt,
vet der lebn zayn zunik.

❉

The sins of the children are visited upon the parents.

Di zind fun di kinder, trogn di eltern.

Through a bad child,
parents bear sin.

Durkh a shlekhte kind, kumen eltern tsu zind.

When children are
young, their parents talk
of their brilliance;
when parents are old,
their children talk
about the foolishness
of their parents.

Ven di kinder zaynen yung, dertseyln di eltern
zeyere khokhmes; ven di eltern vern alt dertseyln di
kinder di narishkaytn fun di eltern.

✺

The way you cradle and
rock your children, that's how
they'll grow.

Azoy vi men vigt ayn, azoy vigt men oys.

✺